Harvesting Hope

Harvesting Hope

THE STORY OF CESAR CHAVEZ

KATHLEEN KRULL

ILLUSTRATED BY YUYI MORALES

HARCOURT, INC.
San Diego   New York   London
Printed in Singapore

Until Cesar Chavez was ten, every summer night was like a fiesta. Relatives swarmed onto the ranch for barbecues with watermelon, lemonade, and fresh corn. Cesar and his brothers, sisters, and cousins settled down to sleep outside, under netting to keep mosquitoes out. But who could sleep—with uncles and aunts singing, spinning ghost stories, and telling magical tales of life back in Mexico?

Cesar thought the whole world belonged to his family. The eighty acres of their ranch were an island in the shimmering Arizona desert, and the starry skies were all their own.

Many years earlier, Cesar's grandfather had built their spacious adobe house to last forever, with walls eighteen inches thick. A vegetable garden, cows, and chickens supplied all the food they could want. With hundreds of cousins on farms nearby, there was always someone to play with. Cesar's best friend was his brother Richard; they never spent a day apart.

Cesar was so happy at home that he was a little afraid when school started. On his first day, he grabbed the seat next to his older sister, Rita. The teacher moved him to another seat—and Cesar flew out the door and ran home. It took three days of coaxing for him to return to school and take his place with the other first graders.

Cesar was stubborn, but he was not a fighter. His mother cautioned her children against fighting, urging them to use their minds and mouths to work out conflicts.

Then, in 1937, the summer Cesar was ten, the trees around the ranch began to wilt. The sun baked the farm soil rock hard. A drought was choking the life out of Arizona. Without water for the crops, the Chavez family couldn't make money to pay its bills.

There came a day when Cesar's mother couldn't stop crying. In a daze, Cesar watched his father strap their possessions onto the roof of their old car. After a long struggle, the family no longer owned the ranch. They had no choice but to join the hundreds of thousands of people fleeing to the green valleys of California to look for work.

Cesar's old life had vanished. Now he and his family were migrants—working on other people's farms, crisscrossing California, picking whatever fruits and vegetables were in season.

When the Chavez family arrived at the first of their new homes in California, they found a battered old shed. Its doors were missing and garbage covered the dirt floor. Cold, damp air seeped into their bedding and clothes. They shared water and outdoor toilets with a dozen other families, and overcrowding made everything filthy. The neighbors were constantly fighting, and the noise upset Cesar. He had no place to play games with Richard. Meals were sometimes made of dandelion greens gathered along the road.

Cesar swallowed his bitter homesickness and worked alongside his family. He was small and not very strong, but still a fierce worker. Nearly every crop caused torment. Yanking out beets broke the skin between his thumb and index finger. Grapevines sprayed with bug-killing chemicals made his eyes sting and his lungs wheeze. Lettuce had to be the worst. Thinning lettuce all day with a short-handled hoe would make hot spasms shoot through his back. Farm chores on someone else's farm instead of on his own felt like a form of slavery.

The Chavez family talked constantly of saving enough money to buy back their ranch. But by each sundown, the whole family had earned as little as thirty cents for the day's work. As the years blurred together, they spoke of the ranch less and less.

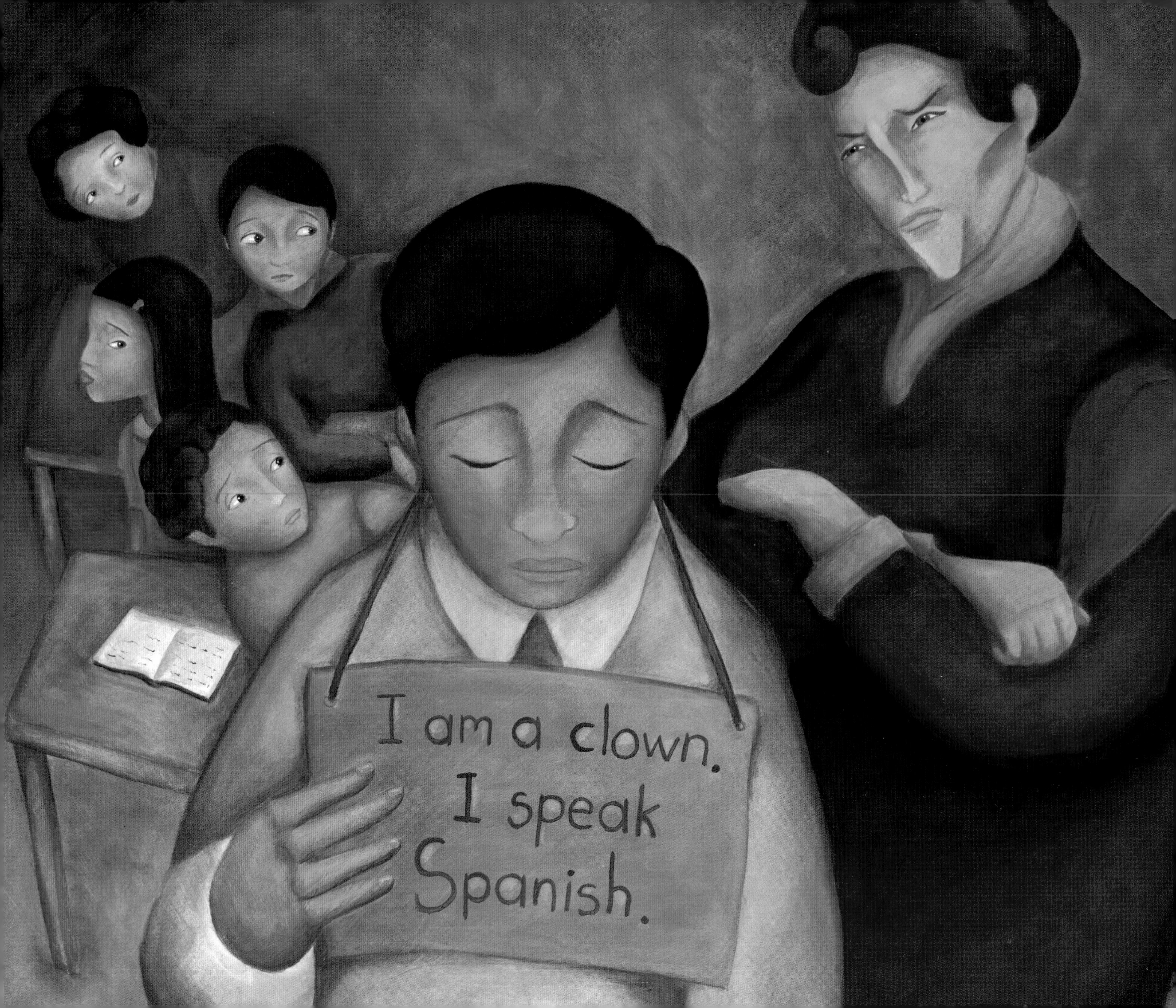
I am a clown.
I speak
Spanish.

SPEAK ENGLISH

The towns weren't much better than the fields. WHITE TRADE ONLY signs were displayed in many stores and restaurants. None of the thirty-five schools Cesar attended over the years seemed like a safe place, either. Once, after Cesar broke the rule about speaking English at all times, a teacher hung a sign on him that read, I AM A CLOWN. I SPEAK SPANISH. He came to hate school because of the conflicts, though he liked to learn. Even he considered his eighth-grade graduation a miracle. After eighth grade he dropped out to work in the fields full-time.

His lack of schooling embarrassed Cesar for the rest of his life, but as a teenager he just wanted to put food on his family's table. As he worked, it disturbed him that landowners treated their workers more like farm tools than human beings. They provided no clean drinking water, rest periods, or access to bathrooms. Anyone who complained was fired, beaten up, or sometimes even murdered.

So, like other migrant workers, Cesar was afraid and suspicious whenever outsiders showed up to try to help. How could they know about feeling so powerless? Who could battle such odds?

Yet Cesar had never forgotten his old life in Arizona and the jolt he'd felt when it was turned upside down. Farmwork did not have to be this miserable.

Reluctantly, he started paying attention to the outsiders. He began to think that maybe there was hope. And in his early twenties, he decided to dedicate the rest of his life to fighting for change.

Again he crisscrossed California, this time to talk people into joining his fight. At first, out of every hundred workers he talked to, perhaps one would agree with him. One by one— this was how he started.

At the first meeting Cesar organized,
a dozen women gathered. He sat quietly
in a corner. After twenty minutes, everyone
started wondering when the organizer
would show up. Cesar thought he might
die of embarrassment.

"Well, I'm the organizer," he said—and
forced himself to keep talking, hoping to
inspire respect with his new suit and the
mustache he was trying to grow. The women
listened politely, and he was sure they did
so out of pity.

But despite his shyness, Cesar showed a
knack for solving problems. People trusted
him. With workers he was endlessly patient
and compassionate. With landowners he was
stubborn, demanding, and single-minded.
He was learning to be a fighter.

In a fight for justice, he told everyone, truth was a better weapon than violence. "Nonviolence," he said, "takes more guts." It meant using imagination to find ways to overcome powerlessness.

More and more people listened.

One night, 150 people poured into an old abandoned theater in Fresno. At this first meeting of the National Farm Workers Association, Cesar unveiled its flag—a bold black eagle, the sacred bird of the Aztec Indians.

La Causa—The Cause—was born.

HUELGA

It was time to rebel, and the place was Delano. Here, in the heart of the lush San Joaquin Valley, brilliant green vineyards reached toward every horizon. Poorly paid workers hunched over grapevines for most of each year. Then, in 1965, the vineyard owners cut their pay even further.

Cesar chose to fight just one of the forty landowners, hopeful that others would get the message. As plump grapes drooped, thousands of workers walked off that company's fields in a strike, or *huelga*.

Grapes, when ripe, do not last long.

The company fought back with everything from punches to bullets. Cesar refused to respond with violence. Violence would only hurt *La Causa*. Instead, he organized a march—a march of more than three hundred miles. He and his supporters would walk from Delano to the state capitol in Sacramento to ask for the government's help.

Cesar and sixty-seven others started out one morning. Their first obstacle was the Delano police force, thirty of whose members locked arms to prevent the group from crossing the street. After three hours of arguing— in public—the chief of police backed down. Joyous marchers headed north under the sizzling sun. Their rallying cry was *Sí Se Puede,* or "Yes, It Can Be Done."

The first night, they reached Ducor. The marchers slept outside the tiny cabin of the only person who would welcome them.

Single file they continued, covering an average of fifteen miles a day.
They inched their way through the San Joaquin Valley, while the unharvested
grapes in Delano turned white with mold. Cesar developed painful blisters
right away. He and many others had blood seeping out of their shoes.

The word spread. Along the way, farmworkers offered food and drink
as the marchers passed by. When the sun set, marchers lit candles and kept
going.

Shelter was no longer a problem. Supporters began welcoming them each night with feasts. Every night was a rally. "Our pilgrimage is the match," one speaker shouted, "that will light our cause for all farmworkers to see what is happening here."

Another cried, "We seek our basic, God-given rights as human beings…*¡Viva La Causa!*"

Eager supporters would keep the marchers up half the night talking about change. Every morning, the line of marchers swelled, Cesar always in the lead.

On the ninth day, hundreds marched through Fresno.

The long, peaceful march was a shock to people unaware of how California farmworkers had to live. Now students, public officials, religious leaders, and citizens from everywhere offered help. For the grape company, the publicity was becoming unbearable.

And on the vines, the grapes continued to rot.

In Modesto, on the fifteenth day, an exhilarated crowd celebrated Cesar's thirty-eighth birthday. Two days later, five thousand people met the marchers in Stockton with flowers, guitars, and accordions.

That evening, Cesar received a message that he was sure was a prank. But in case it was true, he left the march and had someone drive him all through the night to a mansion in wealthy Beverly Hills. Officials from the grape company were waiting for him. They were ready to recognize the authority of the National Farm Workers Association, promising a contract with a pay raise and better conditions.

Cesar rushed back to join the march.

On Easter Sunday, when the marchers arrived in Sacramento, the parade was ten-thousand-people strong.

From the steps of the state capitol building, the joyous announcement was made to the public: Cesar Chavez had just signed the first contract for farmworkers in American history.

The parade erupted into a giant fiesta. Crowds swarmed the steps, some people cheering, many weeping. Prancing horses carried men in mariachi outfits. Everyone sang and waved flowers or flags. They made a place of honor for the fifty-seven marchers who had walked the entire journey.

Speaker after speaker, addressing the audience in Spanish and in English, took the microphone. "You cannot close your eyes and your ears to us any longer," cried one. "You cannot pretend that we do not exist."

The crowd celebrated until the sky was full of stars.

The march had taken its toll. Cesar's leg was swollen and he was running a high fever. Gently he reminded everyone that the battle was not over: "It is well to remember there must be courage but also that in victory there must be humility."

Much more work lay ahead, but the victory was stunning. Some of the wealthiest people in the country had been forced to recognize some of the poorest as human beings. Cesar Chavez had won this fight—without violence—and he would never be powerless again.

Cesar Chavez was born near Yuma, Arizona, in 1927. Before he founded the National Farm Workers Association, workers had no way to protect themselves. They had the longest hours, lowest wages, harshest conditions, shortest life spans, and least power of any group of workers in America. "We had never thought," Chavez said, "that we could actually have any say in our lives. We were poor, we knew it, and we were beyond helping ourselves."

After the walk to Sacramento, the longest protest march in U.S. history, Chavez was known to many as a hero. To show his continuing commitment to *La Causa,* he would occasionally stop eating. His hunger strikes would attract publicity from around the world. Flying black eagles began to be printed on grape boxes from the few companies that offered contracts, and much of the public learned to avoid the others.

It took five years—of fasting by Chavez, of jail for him and other leaders, of marches, picketing, and bargaining—before most of the largest Delano grape-growers gave in. Millions of pounds of grapes had rotted, costing growers more than twenty-five million dollars. It was the first successful agricultural strike in U.S. history. Contracts promised better wages, health insurance, and other safeguards.

Forty-five minutes after he signed the last of the grape contracts, Chavez was organizing a strike of lettuce workers elsewhere in California. Putting in eighteen-hour days, always on the move, he won many more fights on behalf of migrants—including the banning of the short-handled hoe, the cause of permanent back injury to thousands of workers.

Chavez credited his mother's teachings as a chief influence. He also took strength from his religious faith, his Mexican heritage, and his heroes—Saint Francis of Assisi; Dr. Martin Luther King Jr., leader of the African American civil rights movement; and Mahatma Gandhi, who led the nonviolent fight for India's independence from Great Britain. Chavez's wife, Helen, provided indispensable help, as did his eight children, other family members, and loyal coworkers.

In 1993, after a hunger strike lasting thirty-six days, Chavez never fully regained his strength. He died in his sleep at age sixty-six. A crowd many times larger than the one that had greeted him in Sacramento attended his funeral in Delano.

Chavez was—and is—controversial. Especially among those resistant to change, he had many enemies and received constant death threats. Even today, some argue about him and his goals, and others have forgotten him or have never heard of him. But many continue to see him as a hero—for his utter sincerity, his belief that peaceful dedication to a cause is more effective than force, and his self-sacrifice in the face of overwhelming odds.

To Helen Foster James—K. K.

To Abuelo Eligio and his grandson Kelly, árbol y semilla—Y. M.

Text copyright © 2003 by Kathleen Krull
Illustrations copyright © 2003 by Yuyi Morales

www.HarcourtBooks.com

Library of Congress Cataloging-in-Publication Data
Krull, Kathleen.
Harvesting hope: the story of Cesar Chavez/Kathleen Krull; illustrated by Yuyi Morales.
p. cm.
Summary: A biography of Cesar Chavez, from age ten when he and his family lived happily on their Arizona ranch, to age thirty-eight when he led a peaceful protest against California migrant workers' miserable working conditions.
1. Chavez, Cesar, 1927– —Juvenile literature.   2. Mexican Americans—Biography—Juvenile literature.
3. Labor leaders—United States—Biography—Juvenile literature.   4. United Farm Workers—History—Juvenile literature.   [1. Chavez, Cesar, 1927–
2. Labor leaders.   3. Mexican Americans—Biography.   4. Migrant labor.   5. United Farm Workers.]   I. Morales, Yuyi, ill.   II. Title.
HD6509.C48K78   2003
331.88'13'092—dc21   2002005096
ISBN 0-15-201437-3

E G H F

The illustrations in this book were done with acrylics, handmade stamps, and computer-created cutouts on BFK Rives Paper.
The display lettering was created by Tom Seibert.
The text type was set in Columbus Bold.
Color separations by Bright Arts Ltd., Hong Kong
Printed and bound by Tien Wah Press, Singapore
This book was printed on totally chlorine-free Enso Stora Matte paper.
Production supervision by Sandra Grebenar and Ginger Boyer
Designed by Judythe Sieck

ACKNOWLEDGMENT:
Special thanks to Daniel Romero and to all those who walked the fields with me,
sharing their knowledge of Cesar and their stories about the struggle of the farmworkers.
—Y. M.